# Ahi to Ziti

## Food from A to Z

Tracy Kompelien

Consulting Editor, Diane Craig, M.A./Reading Specialist

Published by ABDO Publishing Company, 8000 West 78th Street, Edina, Minnesota 55439. Copyright © 2008 by Abdo Consulting Group, Inc. International copyrights reserved in all countries. No part of this book may be reproduced in any form without written permission from the publisher. Super SandCastle™ is a trademark and logo of ABDO Publishing Company.

Printed in the United States.

Editor: Pam Price
Consulting Editor: Diane Craig, M.A./Reading Specialist
Content Developer: Nancy Tuminelly
Cover and Interior Design and Production: Mighty Media
Photo Credits: Shutterstock, Kelly Doudna

Library of Congress Cataloging-in-Publication Data

Kompelien, Tracy, 1975-
  Ahi to ziti : food from A to Z / Tracy Kompelien.
    p. cm. -- (Let's see A to Z)
  ISBN-13: 978-1-59928-880-2
  1. Food--Juvenile literature. I. Title.
  TX355.K665 2007
  641.3--dc22
                                    2007012154

Super SandCastle™ books are created by a team of professional educators, reading specialists, and content developers around five essential components—phonemic awareness, phonics, vocabulary, text comprehension, and fluency—to assist young readers as they develop reading skills and strategies and increase their general knowledge. All books are written, reviewed, and leveled for guided reading, early reading intervention, and Accelerated Reader® programs for use in shared, guided, and independent reading and writing activities to support a balanced approach to literacy instruction.

# About Super Sandcastle™

## Bigger Books for Emerging Readers Grades PreK–3

Created for library, classroom, and at-home use, Super SandCastle™ books support and engage young readers as they develop and build literacy skills and will increase their general knowledge about the world around them. Super SandCastle™ books are part of SandCastle™, the leading PreK-3 imprint for emerging and beginning readers. Super SandCastle™ features a larger trim size for more reading fun.

## Let Us Know

Super SandCastle™ would like to hear your stories about reading this book. What was your favorite page? Was there something hard that you needed help with? Share the ups and downs of learning to read. We want to hear from you! Send us an e-mail.

sandcastle@abdopublishing.com

Contact us for a complete list of SandCastle™, Super SandCastle™, and other nonfiction and fiction titles from ABDO Publishing Company.

www.abdopublishing.com • 8000 West 78th Street Edina, MN 55439 • 800-800-1312 • 952-831-1632 fax

This fun and informative series employs illustrated definitions to introduce emerging readers to an alphabet of words in various topic areas. Each page combines words with corresponding images and descriptive sentences to encourage learning and knowledge retention. AlphagalorZ inspires young readers to find out more about the subjects that most interest them!

The "Guess What?" feature expands the reading and learning experience by offering additional information and fascinating facts about specific words or concepts. The "More Words" section provides additional related A to Z vocabulary words that develop and increase reading comprehension.

These books are appropriate for library, classroom, and home use.

# A a

## Ahi

Ahi is a Hawaiian name for yellowfin and bigeye tuna.

Sushi is sometimes made with ahi.

sushi roll with tuna

## Asparagus

Asparagus is a green vegetable.

Asparagus is very good for you and is high in vitamins K, C, and A.

# Bagel

**Bagels** are doughnut-shaped rolls.

They are often eaten with cream cheese.

# Banana

**Bananas** grow on trees.

They are picked when they are green and turn yellow as they ripen.

**Guess what?** Bagels are boiled before they are baked. This creates their chewy crust.

## Cocoa

**Cocoa** is made from cacao beans.

**Cocoa** is the main ingredient in chocolate.

## Cucumber

**Cucumbers** are fruit.

They can be eaten raw on a salad!

**Guess what?** Pickles are cucumbers that have been canned in vinegar and seasonings.

# Dill

dried dill

fresh dill

Dill is an herb.

Dill has a distinct flavor and is used to make pickles.

# Dandelion

Dandelion greens taste slightly bitter.

They can be added to salad or sauteed.

**Guess what?** Dandelions may look like pretty flowers, but many people think of dandelions as weeds!

# Eggplant

**Eggplant** is usually purple, but yellow and white **eggplants** are also common.

# Endive

**Endive** is a plant that is sometimes eaten in salads.

The leaf edges are very curly!

**Guess what?** Eggplants, tomatoes, and potatoes are in the nightshade family.

# Figs

Figs are like big raisins.

They are soft, sweet, and chewy.

In ancient times, figs were thought to be sacred.

# F f Focaccia

Focaccia is a round, flat Italian bread.

It is usually topped with olive oil and herbs.

# Garbanzo

**Garbanzo** beans are also known as chickpeas.

They are larger than peas and are brown.

# Grape

**Grapes** are smooth berries that grow on vines.

These sweet berries can be green, red, or purple.

**Guess what?** Hummus is made from mashed garbanzo beans.

# Hazelnut

Most of the world's hazelnuts are grown in Turkey.

Hazelnuts are also called filberts.

# Honey

Honey is a sweet, thick fluid that is made by bees.

Honey is a natural sweetener.

# Ice Cream

**Ice cream** is a popular dessert.

It is made with cream or milk, sugar, flavoring, and often eggs.

## Icing

**Icing** is a sweet mixture used on cake and cupcakes.

**Icing** can be made in many flavors and can be thick or thin.

**Guess what?** In the United States, vanilla is the most popular flavor of ice cream.

# Jam

**Jam** is a spread made from fruit pulp and fruit juice.

Jelly is similar to **jam** but is smooth because it does not contain fruit pulp.

# Jalapeño

**Jalapeño** peppers are chili peppers.

They can spice up any meal!

**Guess what?** If you eat something spicy, a sip of milk will cool the burn, but water won't!

# Kidney Bean

You will find kidney beans in chili and different soups.

Kidney beans are red and have a lot of flavor.

# Kebab

A kebab consists of small pieces of food stuck on a wooden skewer.

# Lime

A lime is a small, green citrus fruit.

Limes contain vitamin C.

They are sour tasting.

# Leek

A leek is a stalk that tastes like a mild onion.

**Guess what?** British sailors were called "limeys" because they ate limes to prevent scurvy, a disease caused by lack of vitamin C.

# Mango

A mango is a tropical fruit that is yellow and red when ripe.

Mangoes are very sweet.

# Mustard

Mustard is a thick yellow or brown sauce that is used as a condiment.

Mustard is made from the ground seeds of the mustard plant.

# Nutmeg

Nutmeg is the seed of the nutmeg tree.

Each seed is about one inch long.

Ground nutmeg is used in baked goods and egg nog!

# N n

# Nut

A nut is a dry fruit or seed that grows inside a shell.

Nuts are often salted and roasted but can also be eaten raw.

**Guess what?** The lacy outer covering of nutmeg is also a spice. It is called mace.

## Olive

**Olive** are oily, bitter fruits that grow on trees.

Be careful when eating **olives**, they contain hard pits!

## Okra

Green **okra** pods can be stewed, baked, or fried.

They are included in many Southern delicacies, such as gumbo.

# Pomegranate

Hundreds of seeds are inside each pomegranate.

They have a lot of vitamin C.

# Pumpkin

A pumpkin is a sweet-tasting squash.

People use pumpkin to make soup, cookies, bread, pasta, filling, pies, and more!

# Q q

## Quinoa

Quinoa is a grain.

It is used to make soups and side dishes.

## Quiche

Quiche may look like pie, but it is savory not sweet!

Its crust is filled with eggs, cheese, and meat or vegetables.

**Guess what?** Many vegetarians eat quinoa because it has a lot of protein!

# Rosemary

**Rosemary** is an herb that is in the mint family.

It is used to season meat, fish, and vegetables.

# Rhubarb

**Rhubarb** is a vegetable.

**Rhubarb** stalks look like celery but are a deep pink color.

Guess what? Be careful! Rhubarb stalks are edible, but the leaves are toxic and should not be eaten!

# Squash

yellow button squash

**Squash** grow on vines.

There are many different kinds of squash.

# Salsa

**Salsa** is a Mexican relish made with fresh tomatoes, chilis, cilantro, and onion.

**Salsa** can be very spicy, so be sure to try it in small amounts!

**Guess what?** Salsa is also a style of Latin music and dance that originated in Cuba.

# Taffy

**Taffy** is a chewy candy made by boiling a mixture of butter, sugar, and flavorings.

# Taco

A **taco** is a corn or flour tortilla filled with meat, cheese, onions, and salsa.

In Mexico, **taco** stands are everywhere!

Guess what? There really is salt in saltwater taffy!

23

# Ugli Fruit

Ugli fruits resemble tangerines or grapefruits.

Ugli fruit is sweet and tangy, much like other citrus fruits.

# Udon

Udon is similar to spaghetti, but it is Japanese.

Udon are the thickest Japanese noodles.

# Vanilla

Vanilla beans are the seed pods of vanilla orchids.

Vanilla extract is made by soaking vanilla beans in alcohol and water.

# Vinaigrette

Vinaigrette is a sauce that is used on salads and other dishes.

Vinaigrette is made of vinegar, oil, and seasonings.

# W

## Watermelon

**Watermelon** is a type of melon.

Many people enjoy it on a hot summer day!

## Wild Rice

**Wild rice** isn't really rice! It is actually the seed of a marsh grass.

**Wild rice** is used in soups or served as a side dish.

**Guess what?** A watermelon can weigh up to 35 pounds!

# Xacuti

**Xacuti** is a spicy Indian curry dish.

It is made with roasted coconut and many spices, including white poppy seeds and red chilis.

# Y y

## Yeast

Yeast is a living organism!

Without yeast, bread would not rise.

## Yam

Yams are roots that mainly have a sweet flavor.

In the United States, sweet potatoes are often called yams even though sweet potatoes and yams come from different plants.

**? Guess what ?** Jewel yams and garnet yams are really sweet potatoes!

# Zest

Zest is the outer part of a citrus fruit rind.

Zest gives food a citrus flavor.

# Ziti

Ziti is a tube-shaped pasta.

Baked ziti is a popular Italian dish!

# Glossary

bean – a seed or a pod that you can eat. Also, something that looks like a bean but is not a bean, such as coffee beans and vanilla beans.

citrus – a fruit such as an orange, lemon, or lime that grows on a warm-climate evergreen and has a thick skin and a juicy pulp.

condiment – something that adds flavor to food, such as a sauce or a spice.

crust – the pastry shell under and sometimes over a pie.

curry – an Indian dish flavored with strong spices.

dessert – a sweet food, such as fruit, ice cream, or pastry, served after a meal.

edible – safe to eat.

fluid – a substance that flows easily and takes the shape of its container.

herb – a scented plant used to flavor food or make medicine.

mixture – a combination of several different things.

**pulp** – the soft, juicy part of a fruit or vegetable.

**raw** – not cooked.

**rind** – the tough outer layer of something.

**root** – the part of a plant that grows underground.

**savory** – having a strong, pleasing flavor that is not sweet.

**skewer** – a long wood or metal pin used to hold pieces of food while they cook.

**spice** – a plant part with a pleasing smell that is used to flavor food. Cinnamon, pepper, and cloves are some kinds of spices.

**sushi** – a small amount of cold rice topped with raw seafood or vegetables and sometimes wrapped in seaweed.

**vegetable** – the edible part of a plant grown for food.

**weed** – a plant that is growing where it shouldn't.

**wild** – living or growing in nature without human help or attention.

# More Food Talk!

## Can you learn about these foods too?

| | | |
|---|---|---|
| almond | falafel | lettuce |
| anchovy | French toast | macaroni |
| anise | ginger | nectarine |
| bacon | Gorgonzola | pancake |
| baklava | granola | papaya |
| cabbage | grapefruit | pesto |
| cantaloupe | hamburger | potato |
| date | jelly bean | radish |
| Dijon mustard | jerky | raspberry |
| dirty rice | jicama | spinach |
| duck sauce | juniper berry | tomato |
| enchilada | kale | turmeric |
| English muffin | ketchup | wasabi |